THE

PERFECT
NEGOTIATION

THE

PERFECT

NEGOTIATION

GAVIN KENNEDY

WINGS BOOKS
New York • *Avenel, New Jersey*

For John

Copyright © 1992 by Gavin Kennedy

This 1994 edition is published by Wings Books,
distributed by Random House Value Publishing, Inc.,
40 Engelhard Avenue, Avenel, New Jersey 07001,
by arrangement with Random Century,
an imprint of Random House UK Limited.

Random House
New York • Toronto • London • Sydney • Auckland

Printed and bound in the United States of America

Library of Congress Cataloging-in-Publication Data

Kennedy, Gavin.
    The perfect negotiation / Gavin Kennedy.
        p.   cm.
    ISBN 0-517-10143-2
    1. Negotiation.   I. Title.
    BF637.N4K46   1994
    302.3—dc20   94-6703
                                                    CIP

8 7 6 5 4 3 2 1

CONTENTS

PREFACE

The Perfect Negotiation summarizes the approach to negotiation with which I have been closely associated for over twenty years. The contents appear largely as they are presented in The NEGOTIATE Workshop, which features the Four Phases of Preparation, Debate, Propose and Bargain. Indeed the workshop materials, particularly The Negotiators Notebook, have been extensively used to compile this summary, as has my best-selling book, *Everything is Negotiable* (Century Business 1982; 1990).

As ever my colleagues have contributed to my work over the years, among them John Benson (Chairman of Negotiate Ltd and Senior Partner of PDB), whose collaboration with me has been typically unselfish, open and creative since we first took on the task of training negotiators in 1972. I am sure none of my other colleagues and collaborators will demur if I select him for special mention and state that this book is for him. Nobody in their negotiating approach and skills (both strategic and tactical) gets closer than John in their practical work to the principles outlined in *The Perfect Negotiation*.

Readers interested in discovering for themselves how we put the principles of *The Perfect Negotiation* to work in our training and consulting work should send their business cards to: NEGOTIATE LTD, 22 Braid Avenue, Edinburgh, EH10 6EE, Scotland, or call on 031 452 8404 (Fax 031 452 8388). A brochure will be sent by return detailing our public and in-house training workshops. I am also interested in your views on *The Perfect Negotiation*.

EX BONA FIDE NEGOTIARI
Gavin Kennedy   Edinburgh 1992

INTRODUCTION

There are several approaches to improving our negotiating skills.

Some people advocate "sink or swim" strategies by sending untrained negotiators to jump in at the deep end. While this approach can sort out the "doers" from the "viewers," it is also a hit and miss use of talent and opportunity.

You can also read about how experts have negotiated mega deals in recent corporate history and send for some relevant tips for your own deals. If what you read about is not relevant, you are no further forward.

Likewise, you can listen to the "streetwise" on how to win through intimidation, bluffs and tactical manipulation. Numerous texts extol the manipulation approach but all suffer from three weaknesses: you forget the appropriate ploy; you select the wrong ploy; your situation was not covered in the text. And even where none of these weaknesses apply there is another problem with manipulation —it alienates those with whom you want to do business.

Some other approaches provide extremely useful insights into negotiation practice, but it is not sufficient to rely on their approach. Selecting criteria for a settlement, for example, is helpful in some negotiations but not in others. If the parties cannot agree on the appropriate criteria, because the criteria will determine the nature of the settlement, we are back where we started.

None of these approaches will necessarily lead you to a lasting improvement in your negotiating skills because they do not provide you with an approach that is at once specific enough to guide you in detailed circumstances and general enough to cover every circumstance.

The Perfect Negotiation presents the Four Phases of negotiation which apply to all negotiations, irrespective of the people involved, the interests they serve, the culture and personalities of the negotiators, the issues at stake or the place or circumstances.

Distinguishing between the phases that are common to all negotiators, by identifying the skills appropriate to each phase, will enable the negotiator, irrespective of his/her previous level of performance, to improve his/her performance dramatically in a short period of time.

Of course further practice is required if the improvement in performance is to become lasting rather than transitory. But given that much of what is required to improve our performance is in fact quite simple and straightforward it is not too difficult to find circumstances and contexts where we can practice on a regular basis.

The Perfect Negotiation provides you with the basic situations of the negotiating process. It identifies the skills that work and the pitfalls to avoid. Apply its precepts in your daily negotiations at work, at home, in the community and with your colleagues and you will achieve more of what you want in less time and with less stress than, perhaps, you have been used to up to now.

WHAT IS NEGOTIATION?

INTRODUCTION

All resources are finite. Animals, and some humans, fight for food, mates and territory, using various forms of dominance and display to decide who gets how much of what and when they get it.

Using, or even threatening, violence can only redistribute wealth, it cannot create it.

Through civilization humans have developed the capacity to distribute the basics of food, mates and territory, and today's vast array of products and services, by means other than violence or the threat of violence.

One of the methods we use is called negotiation.

DEFINITIONS

Negotiation is the process by which we pursue the terms for getting what we want from people who want something from us.

It can also be described as "a process for resolving conflict between two or more parties whereby both or all modify their demands to achieve a mutually acceptable compromise."

Another definition is "a process of adjusting both parties' views of their ideal outcome to an attainable outcome."

Negotiation is a synonym for trading; for exchanging things we have that others want, for things we want from them. Implicit in every negotiation is the statement: "Give me some of what I want, and I will give you some of what you want."

ALTERNATIVES TO NEGOTIATION

Conflict cannot always be resolved by negotiation. There are alternatives including "agreeing to disagree" (e.g. a potential customer deciding not to buy at the price asked).

There are several alternatives to negotiation, all of them familiar to every adult, and to many children, who are used to switching between them to get what they want:

Persuasion ("Our services are good value")

Persuasion is often tried first when people want something, but it is seldom successful when their interests clash. All selling skills are persuasion skills; if you already have double glazing you are unlikely to be persuaded to buy a new set of windows.

Giving in ("OK, I'll cut prices by 30 per cent")

Giving in is an option when the odds are overwhelming, or the issue is trivial. It involves giving in to your opponent's wants, or doing without your own. We will give in every time we visit a supermarket for groceries. We normally accept the prices on the goods, pay them at the checkout and take them home. Giving in and negotiation do not go well together. It encourages difficult negotiators to be more difficult.

Coercion ("Meet my demands, or else!")

In some circumstances you might coerce people to do what you want, but this risks long-term relationships and provokes hostility and revenge. Coercion in a negotiation context is unwise. It hardens attitudes and leads to damaging counter-blows.

Problem solving ("How can we avoid this problem happening again?")
Where all parties recognize that they share a problem, as well as trust each other, it might be possible to use problem-solving techniques.

Instruction ("Take this package to the post office")
Instruction is effective in certain cases. An example is the employer/employee relationship where instructions are accepted by the employee, in specific areas, in return for consideration. They may, however, obey resentfully and await an opportunity to "get their own back."

Arbitration ("Which is fairest, my or her proposals?")
Arbitration is an option in cases where agreement cannot be reached. It can, nevertheless, be unpopular because it reduces the negotiator's power and because the parties can renege if they are not legally bound to comply with the agreement reached.

ALL METHODS HAVE A ROLE TO PLAY

- No method of decision making is superior to another in all circumstances
- Each is appropriate in some circumstances but not in others
- When negotiating it is not normally advisable to give in as this tends to encourage further demands
- Likewise, coercion is risky when negotiating, as it can severely damage the relationship between negotiators
- Choose the most suitable method for the circumstances

No method of getting what you want is superior to any of the others
They all have a role to play in some circumstances where they would fail in others. *The Perfect Negotiation* is con-

cerned with the techniques of negotiation as a method you can use to get what you want.

WHEN IS IT APPROPRIATE TO NEGOTIATE?

- Not always
- When we are given no choice
- When we need each other's consent
- When it is the only way to get what we want
- When the outcome is uncertain
- When the stakes justify our time and effort

THE FOUR PHASES OF NEGOTIATION

INTRODUCTION

All negotiations, no matter what the issues, the history, the culture or the context, can be analyzed in terms of the four phases of negotiation. These main phases were identified from the analysis of actual industrial relations negotiations from 1972–4. They proved to be a helpful training tool, as well as a useful operational tool, for negotiators in various business, personal and international contexts. Most negotiation skill programs now use some or other version of the four phases—not always acknowledging their source—which is a suitable testimony to their relevance.

WHAT IS "PERFECT NEGOTIATION?"

The concept of perfect negotiation is a practical framework through which a trainee negotiator can understand, and cultivate, the necessary skills to conduct successful negotiations.

In this way, the negotiation process is divided into the four main phases through which it will progress before an agreement is reached. These phases are differentiated from each other by the different sets of skills relevant to each one.

A negotiator may fail to exploit these phases as a result of inexperience, lack of training or simple lack of practice. When agreement is eventually reached it is unlikely to represent the best deal possible. It is for this reason that the skills associated with the phases are emphasized.

THE FOUR MAIN PHASES OF NEGOTIATION
Prepare—What do you want?

• Decide what you want and prioritize (value) your wants

Debate—What do they want?

• Disclose what you want but not the terms on which you might settle
• Ask open questions and listen to the answers
• Listen for signals, which indicate a willingness to consider movement

Propose—What could you trade?

• Use "if . . . then" language. (If they meet some of your wants, then you might consider meeting some of their wants)
• Keep quiet and wait for a response
• Do not interrupt proposals

Bargain—What will you trade?

• Trade wants to agree to specific solutions
• Always conditional "if . . . then"
• Record what has been agreed

POINTS TO REMEMBER

• All negotiations have a common structure
• Negotiators are always in one or other of the four phases common to all negotiations
• Identifying the phase you are in helps you to move the negotiations forward

DIVERSIONS AND INTERRUPTIONS

Negotiations are often messy, involve many diversions and interruptions, and do not always move forward in a tidy fashion from preparation to agreement. Fortunately, however, this does not weaken the four phase approach because it was from the real world of negotiating, with all its complexities, that the original analysis identified the phases and the sub-steps that link them.

FLEXIBILITY OF THE FOUR PHASES

It is perfectly acceptable to go backwards and forwards between the phases. For example, while some preparation is completed before the first face-to-face meeting, additional preparation might be necessary because of what you discover once you meet the other negotiators. While debate may be a prelude to a proposal, the proposal may lead to more debate—before you get to another proposal! And so it goes on. For example, asking a question about a proposal or a bargain returns you to the debate phase.

We do not necessarily negotiate in a strict order from phase 1 to phase 4. It is possible to start with debate (phase 2) to learn what is wanted and then to adjourn to prepare (phase 1) our response. Some negotiations begin with proposals (phase 3) and then go on to a debate (phase 2). When a question is asked to clarify a bargain (phase 4), we are back in debate (phase 2). During negotiations we might return to preparation (phase 1) several times. For each phase there are techniques that work and others that do not.

All negotiations involve varying combinations of the four phases. Knowing which phase you are in enables you to adapt your own behavior to the circumstances.

For each phase there are certain techniques that work and other techniques that do not.

MANAGE YOUR NEGOTIATION

Once you understand the role of the four phases in negotiation you are able to "manage" your negotiations. Instead of relying on nothing more than an instinctive reaction to the other negotiator, you are able to choose how to respond. You know what phase you are in, what actions or reactions on your part will help the phase to move forward and what will hinder progress. You are no longer guessing what to do next in your negotiations because you are able to manage what you are doing.

Whether your opponent is aware of the phases or not makes little difference. If they are aware of them, this will assist both of you to move competently towards a settlement, if one is possible. If they are not aware of the phases their reactions may be comparatively disorganized, or badly managed, but yours will not be and this will give you a negotiating edge.

A proposal is a proposal in any language. Their proposals may be poorly phrased, unconditional or just a one-way demand. Yours will always be conditional. The difference will help to educate them in how to do business: nobody gets what they want unless and until you get offered some of what you want.

They may be stuck in an argument while you prefer to explore each other's wants in a constructive debate. Your understanding of the role of each phase assists your efforts to find a solution. Whether they anxiously work through a phase or stumble through it makes little difference to you. Your approach is a conscious application of effective behavior in each phase. You—and they—will notice the difference.

3

PHASE ONE: HOW TO PREPARE

INTRODUCTION

Preparation, or lack of it, will become immediately apparent as negotiations get under way. A negotiator who arrives poorly prepared is really only in a position to react to events, rather than lead them. As this lack of preparation becomes apparent, the other negotiator will naturally feel strengthened in their position. They will therefore become more confident and committed to their own demands, particularly if it is not appropriate for you to adjourn to prepare properly.

A negotiator must nevertheless avoid using preparation time to rehearse a dogmatic defense of any given position, however deeply held, or to adopt an aggressive approach to the other negotiator's position. Constructive preparation is vital.

DEFINING YOUR WANTS

You will negotiate to get what you want. In the preparation phase you will decide or confirm what you want. Hence, the question you should ask yourself is: what do I want to happen as a result of this negotiation? The answer will be a list of your wants.

Merely quantifying what you want is obviously not an automatic guarantee that you are going to get it. In the course of the negotiation you will have to modify your own wants, to a greater or lesser extent, to take account of the competing wants of the other negotiator.

It also is worth noting that opening negotiations may

involve the re-opening of previously settled issues: in the course of the negotiation for an overall advantage it is possible to lose some items which hitherto may have been taken for granted.

MUTUAL OBJECTIVES

In pursuing your own objectives through negotiation you must, of course, give consideration to the other party's objectives, and their approach in attaining them. Establishing the other party's wants and gauging their priorities can be difficult. Particularly so, as it may be in their interests to conceal any such priorities and convince you that their demands are all of equal importance. You cannot balk at such "bluffing" ploys, however, if you yourself are inclined to take this approach. The other party's wants are obviously of some importance, but they are only really of significance insofar as they influence the attainment of your own objectives.

Through negotiation you might get what you want on their terms, or they might get what they want on your terms, or both of you might get some of your wants on each other's terms.

WHAT IS THE NEGOTIATION ABOUT?

All negotiations take place in a context which influences the negotiator's behaviors and their aspirations, the types of issues that are addressed and the range of possible outcomes.

WHAT ISSUES HAVE TO BE ADDRESSED?

An issue is anything over which the negotiators have discretion. For example, issues could include the price of a product, the quantity available, where a country's boundary line runs, how loose or tight a contract clause must be and so on. Through negotiation, issues become the decisions of the parties to the agreement.

WHAT DO YOU WANT?

Wants are preferences in respect of the issues. They are the decisions you prefer to arrive at, though what you want may have to be modified as a result of accommodating the other negotiator's wants. For example: I may want to pay a lower price for your business because of the uncertainty about future profits, while you may want a higher price because you wish to retire in a state of affluence. Through negotiation we might be able to find a way to meet both our wants (e.g. a purchase price in two tiers, one on my acquiring the business, which meets my concerns, the other when its true profits are proven, which meet your ambitions).

List and prioritize wants

For every issue, you should write down what you want. You can be as vague or specific as you need and for the moment you need not concern yourself with what the other negotiator might want.

Now assess how important each of these wants is to you. In short, prioritize your wants. Some wants will be more important than others, some wants you may not be sure about just yet. You may use any categories of importance that you find convenient, such as high, medium and low:

- *High importance:* those that you must get if you are to agree at all. These represent the "bottom line" or "limit position"; the objectives without which a negotiator is not prepared to reach any agreement
- *Medium importance:* those objectives that you would prefer to attain if you could, but which are not critical
- *Low importance:* those objectives that you would like to attain if you could, but would not let a failure to get them jeopardize the deal

Evaluate wants

Next you must assign ranges of possible values to each of the issues you have prioritized. For example, you may set a quantitative range, such as: "$100 to $150." You may equally set a qualitative range, such as "will deliver by Friday" to "use best efforts to deliver by Friday." This requirement is based on the notion that negotiators do not enter the negotiations exactly where they intend to settle—if they did this would imply that there was no movement possible and the negotiation would degenerate into a battle of wills or a power struggle. Negotiating from fixed and inflexible positions is extremely difficult. Despite being easily avoidable, it remains the most common cause of deadlock between negotiators. Giving yourself a range gives you flexibility as well as a greater chance of reaching an agreement.

ENTRY AND EXIT POSITIONS

Hence, you will tend to enter the negotiation with statements of requirements on the issues which you certainly know, and the other negotiator almost certainly will assume, will not be your final position. They will know that wherever you start from, you are probably willing to move somewhat further. The range therefore will begin with an "entry" position and end with an "exit" position. This also provides the rationale for never accepting a negotiator's first offer—because wherever they open there is another position, better for you, where they will go before they close.

Where to enter and where to exit?

Where you enter will depend on the circumstances and on what you believe you can credibly defend to the other negotiator. Unrealistic or overly ambitious objectives should be abandoned prior to the negotiations as putting them forward could antagonize the other negotiator into similarly unrealistic demands. Where you exit will also depend on the circumstances and on what options you have in case you cannot reach agreement.

If you are sure you have many alternative options, your entry point might be relatively ambitious and your exit point relatively close to where you began. If you are not so sure of your strengths, or are convinced that you have few alternative options (few customers, fewer opportunities) you are likely to enter relatively "softly" and be prepared to exit even more "softly" if you have to. Nevertheless, it is a common failing for diffident negotiators to err on the side of caution, aiming lower rather than higher (they often negotiate with themselves first!)

RECORD PREPARATION DETAILS

The details of your preparation can be recorded on a single sheet of paper. The detail you wish to go into will depend on the importance of the negotiation. No matter how short your time, however, some consideration of the issues to be decided will automatically improve your negotiation performance:

- What you want from the negotiation
- The relative importance you attach to your wants
- How you would present your wants, in the form of a range from your entry position to your exit position

Effective handling of face-to-face interaction, the debate phase, will do much to consolidate the advantages gained from improved preparation.

HOW TO PREPARE—EXAMPLE

A manufacturer uses a specialized machine tool for some high-quality components. A problem has emerged with the availability of the machine due to some recurring maintenance fault, delays in the supplier's technicians arriving to correct the fault, and errors on the part of the operators.

The manufacturer has arranged a meeting with the supplier to resolve the problems. It is anticipated that the meeting will lead to negotiation. Independent of this situation, the supplier had already approached the manufacturer with a request to increase prices on the grounds that the maintenance contract was unprofitable.

What might the manufacturer's negotiator do in preparation for the meeting? Apart from collecting recent data on the machine's unavailability and the reasons for each incident, the negotiator would begin to assess the question: What do we want?

Negotiation		Relative	Range	
Issues	Wants	Importance	Entry	Exit
1. Machine availability	Maximized	High	100%	70%
2. Service delays	Minimized	Medium	3-hour call out	24 hours
3. Operator errors	Minimized	Low	Free training by supplier	Training

CHECKLIST FOR PREPARATION

- What do you want to happen as a result of this negotiation?
- What are the negotiable issues?
- What do you want for each issue?
- Rank each want by its importance to you
- High—absolutely critical—certain no deal
- Medium—important but not critical
- Low—like to achieve but would not sacrifice deal if not obtained
- What are your Entry and Exit limits?
- Entry terms should be credible
- Exit terms are your "walking away" positions

- All prepared positions are subject to revision if circumstances suggest changes are advisable

Common mistakes to avoid

- Not finding time to decide what you want
- Confusing "let's hear what they have to say" with preparation
- Being unrealistic when deciding on your Entry and Exit points
- Not prioritizing your wants
- Not setting a range for each want

4

PHASE TWO: HOW TO DEBATE

INTRODUCTION

Debate is the most common form of interaction between negotiators. It accounts for an estimated 80 per cent of time spent in negotiation.

This makes debate a key area for self-improvement because by your conduct in debate with other negotiators you can slow down, hinder, deadlock or alternatively promote a settlement. This is because you can control two things during debate; how you present yourself and how you react to the other negotiator (no matter how they are behaving).

Your approach to debate will influence the progress and outcome of the negotiation. This will not just be at a particular stage, either, as the debate phase will continue throughout the negotiation as a whole.

Coping with debate, getting it to work in favor of your negotiating objectives and not against them, will significantly improve your performance as a negotiator.

USING DEBATE TO GAUGE THE OTHER NEGOTIATOR'S VIEWS

Preparation will have clarified your own standpoint on the issues. You now have to gauge the other negotiator's views. Preparation will also have included conjecture on your part which you will now have the opportunity to test.

The other negotiator will normally need little encouragement to disclose their opinions. They will represent their entry position, and all successive "current" positions, as their exit position as far as you are concerned.

The more you can find out about their position—by

questioning and clarification—the more information you can gain about their commitment to their position and the direction in which they may be prepared to move.

Debate provides a crucial opportunity to glean information about the other negotiator's objectives and attitudes. In this way you can gauge their commitment and identify their interests and intentions; equally important, you will discover their inhibitions. An interest will encourage someone to say "Yes," an inhibition will encourage them to say "No." Neither factor will be immediately obvious to you, and you will initially be reliant upon assumptions. Debate will therefore give you the opportunity to test these assumptions. Foreknowledge of another party's plans, wants or objectives will also offer you the chance to test their candor or basic honesty.

Effective use of debating time should allow you to explore each other's inhibitions as well as your own. Creating this open dialogue between both parties will probably have one of two consequences. It will either acknowledge the mutual benefits of negotiating a settlement or it will demonstrate that a settlement is neither possible nor desirable.

If you concentrate on the task of debate—to find out what the other negotiator wants and let them know what you want—you will avoid disruptive diversions and destructive argument.

FEATURES OF DESTRUCTIVE ARGUMENT

Destructive argument is a temptation at this phase because it helps prevent too close an examination of opening positions. It is an all-too-common feature of many negotiations, and is most likely to arise where parties are highly committed, anxious or angry, even. A prime example would be the unhelpful practice of interrupting. A simple, yet fundamental, step that you can take to improve your performance in negotiations is to dispense with the habit of interrupting other people.

Other features of destructive argument, to be avoided, include the following:

- Regularly point-scoring on issues
- Attacking or blaming somebody for a problem
- Sarcasm and other forms of disrepect
- Personal insults
- Ascribing ulterior motives to other people
- Not listening to what others are saying
- Rising to provocation

Consequences of destructive argument
Few people, for example, can resist point-scoring—reminding the other party of their past failures.

The blame and attack/defense cycles are well-established elements of destructive argument. When someone is attacked they will instinctively defend themselves, however irrelevant the attack is to the main objectives of the negotiation. Attempts to apportion blame will provoke either spontaneous resistance or efforts to retaliate by passing the blame back to you.

As an attack/defense cycle proceeds, emotional tension and personal attacks are evident and interpersonal relationships suffer damage as a result.

Negotiators' inhibitions, including their fears and concerns about your intentions, are reinforced by destructive argument. Inhibitions hinder negotiation and can even obstruct an agreement which is mutually advantageous.

To someone wholly concerned with winning, any movement—no matter how minor—is a loss. The result of such behavior can only be to drive the negotiators apart.

REDUCE TENSION
Negotiations often begin with a degree of tension present. This can be because of the history of the relationship: warring nations, poor industrial relations, failures to perform past or current contracts, squabbling relatives, etc. It can

also be because the negotiators do not know each other, or are uncertain of what is about to be decided. If tension is present, avoiding it worsening into outright hostility is imperative.

Negotiators can do a lot to reduce tension by what they say and how they speak to each other. You can help yourself reduce tension if you remember that your sole task in debate is basically to assess what the other negotiator wants and to inform them of what you want.

Establish rapport

You can begin by establishing rapport with the other negotiator. Rapport establishes your relationship. It sets the tone of the relationship in the first few minutes. Your tone can work against you if you appear hostile (because you feel angry). You can also undermine your negotiating position by too subservient a tone in which you are so desperate to be friendly that you sacrifice your own wants unilaterally. Therefore:

- Show and earn respect
- Follow culturally-set norms of greeting and non-business talk

Determine the order of business

Next, set an agenda to organize the meeting. This can be done formally in writing or informally with a verbal summary of what you propose to discuss. Always invite amendments and comments on the subjects and their order.

Describe what you are seeking

In describing the broad conclusions you are seeking, reassure the other negotiator(s) by using tactful and nonthreatening terms. For example:

- "I hope at the end of the meeting we have agreed to a financial package that will secure the company's future"
- "Difficult as these problems are, I am willing to look at any constructive proposal we can come up with to solve them"
- "My intention is to see if we can agree on general terms at this meeting, for more detailed discussions later"

You must explain your ideal position before you can expect the other negotiators to move towards it. Each party must know the other's ideal position in order to assess its proximity to their own limit.

Avoid threats

Do not state or imply a threat in your opening remarks. For example:

- "If we cannot reach a sensible settlement here, we may have to consider litigation"

Threats are certain to provoke resentment. Your opposite number does not need to be reminded of the consequences of failure before you start. Threats either produce counter-threats or statements of defiance and are thus likely to lead to argument before negotiations have even begun.

Listen positively

To find out what the other party wants, listen to what they say (the more they talk—and the less you do—at this stage, the better). Ask them questions about what they want, and listen to their answers. Anyone who tells you what they want in negotiation is doing you a favor—so if they launch into a monologue you should listen for clues as to their wants and not feel obliged to interrupt.

You must support positive listening behavior with positive talking behavior—making sure you use the time effectively. One way to do this is to ask open questions which encourage explanation and elaboration by the other negotiator.

USE QUESTIONS

Questions are both underrated and badly-used negotiating tools. Below average negotiators do not ask enough, if any, questions and many negotiators who do ask questions ask the wrong kind in the wrong tone.

Keep doors open if you want to be an effective negotiator. Never say "No," instead ask an open question such as "If we were to agree to your proposal, what would you be willing to offer in return . . . ?" Open questions unlock doors.

Don't disagree—ask your opponent an open question instead. When a negotiator makes a statement that you disagree with, you will achieve little if you tell them they are wrong. While you are explaining why they are wrong, they will be thinking of how to defend themselves, perhaps by raising irrelevant matters, perhaps by attacking you. It is much more effective for you to ask open questions about the basis for the statement that you disagree with and for them either to show their statement to be true (in which case you can change your own position without loss of face), or to show that their own statement is false (in which case they can retract without feeling aggrieved).

Right and wrong questions to ask

Examples of the wrong types of questions to ask include:

- "Are you listening?"
- "Are you serious?"
- "Do you think I am stupid?"
- "Is that your final offer?"

These are tension-inducing questions that are likely to lead you away from an early settlement, perhaps into irretrievable deadlock.

Examples of the right type of questions to ask include:

- "What criterion are you using?"
- "What are your priorities?"
- "How do you calculate those numbers?"
- "How do you feel about these issues?"

These questions seek information using an open question format which normally requires an extended answer, rather than a simple "yes" or "no." By using words like "what," "why," "when," "how," "where" and "who," you invite the other negotiator to explain themselves and to disclose their wants.

When asking open questions it is essential to make considered use of language. "How did you arrive at that conclusion?" should elicit useful details about the other negotiator's reasoning. "Do you think I am stupid?", on the other hand, which you might be equally tempted to say, would provoke a counter-productive emotional defense, telling you nothing.

SUMMARIZING

Before you make any response to a detailed proposal it is a good idea to summarize what they have proposed. You can either ask them to do it, or alternatively go through it yourself, highlighting any implications and their (not your) attitude towards them.

Summarizing is positive behavior. It has many uses:

- Simplifies complex issues
- Helps re-focus wandering negotiations
- Reassures them that they are being taken seriously
- Gives you time to think

ARGUMENTS, PRINCIPLES AND OPINIONS CANNOT BE NEGOTIATED

We can only negotiate proposals and therefore debate is more effective if it informs the negotiators of what each wants, because their proposals will have to address those wants. We cannot negotiate the "truth" or "falsity" of someone's beliefs, values, principles or opinions. These lead only to argument.

MOVEMENT

Parties to a negotiation must move from their current preferred solution to some other acceptable solution if an agreement is to be reached. The negotiator's problem is how to make this happen—how to ensure that movement by one side is reciprocated by movement on the other side. The principal motivations for moving are incentives (benefits of agreeing) and sanctions (penalties for not agreeing). These forces may be explicit (attention being drawn to the consequences of agreeing or disagreeing) or implied.

Negotiation is motivated by self-interest. People negotiate because the other party offers them an incentive or threatens them with a sanction. Without either of these there is no negotiation. If you are satisfied with the *status quo*—have nothing to trade and want nothing on offer— you will not negotiate.

However committed the parties appear to be to their position, and however unwilling to trade, they would not be involved in negotiating if they were not willing to consider moving towards an agreement.

DEADLOCK

Deadlock can occur when both parties rely on the strategy of sticking to their current position until the other is willing to move. If both sides adopt this approach there will be no movement.

Why should a party be unwilling to negotiate? Distrust and tension may be present. One party may see its interests as being best served by resisting change of any kind and maintaining the existing situation. Only if they come to believe that the potential outcome is likely to be an improvement in the existing situation, or less damaging than the possible consequences of the existing situation, will they be willing to negotiate.

Why else is compromise avoided?

Because movement can be interpreted as weakness. If you refuse to move for long enough the other party may ultimately "surrender;" alternatively the negotiation may fail completely.

Inexperienced negotiators often fall into the trap of giving away too much too soon, resulting in an unsatisfactory agreement, or no movement at all, thereby achieving no agreement.

Balancing firmness and flexibility

There is a dilemma faced by all negotiators; how do you suggest flexibility in your entry requirements without giving in? Once you move from a position, there is a danger that one move will follow another, until you have nothing left to negotiate and nothing to show for your movement. Below-average negotiators do not move at all. They try intimidation, with the intention of forcing the other negotiator to give in, or in the hope that they will do so. Effective negotiators, however, listen and watch for signals.

LOOKING FOR SIGNALS

Every negotiation has at least two solutions to the same issue—the solution that meets your wants and the solution that meets the other party's wants. Your strategic task is to arrive at an agreed solution, which almost certainly will be different from either of the two solutions with which the negotiation began. Hence, you look for signals, or signs of a willingness to consider movement.

Signalling behavior provides a method with which to handle movement confidently.

A signal is a means by which parties indicate their willingness to negotiate on something. It is also more than that: it implies a willingness only if it is reciprocated by the other side and not treated as a first step on the slippery slope to surrender.

Advantages of signalling behavior

- Can be used to break the cycle of circular argument
- Allows you to make new proposals without being seen to give in
- Familiar behavior we often use—nothing new to learn

What are signals?
Signals are qualifications attached to a statement. For example:

- "Our normal price is . . ."
  (But we have a different price for special circumstances)
- "It would be extremely difficult . . ."
  (But not necessarily impossible)
- "We do not want to be locked into this deal . . ."
  (We need an escape clause)

The negotiator suggests the possibility of agreement if the other party's proposal is amended in some way. It is an invitation to the other party to move. It says that although the present proposal is unacceptable, it would be negotiable if put in another form.

RESPONDING TO SIGNALS
Signals hint at the possibilities of movement if, and only if, the other negotiator responds positively. At this stage

the category of response is crucial. Of course, if the other negotiator attacks the signaller you can be sure that they will slip back towards argument:

- "I don't care about your normal prices"
- "So after an hour of pretending it was impossible to change the contract, you now agree it can be changed"
- "You are either in the deal totally or there is no deal at all"

Summarize signals

The most effective way to respond to a signal is to confirm what you heard by summarizing what is said to you—even if you do not yet see how the signal helps you—and then encourage the other party to expand on their tentative hints by asking open questions about the signal. For example:

- "Under what circumstances would you consider a non-list price?"
- "How could we make it easier for you to re-examine this clause?"
- "How can we address your concerns about being locked in?"

This type of open question can reveal their wants in greater detail and what wants of yours they might be prepared to meet.

Signalling does not inevitably lead to agreement, nor resolve conflict. It makes negotiation about the issues possible and leads to the possibility of agreement. Signals lead to proposals—they are the bridge between debate and attempts to trade.

ADJOURN

Wherever possible, you should take an adjournment at this point, to consider what you have learned about the other negotiator's wants, and to assess the initial reactions to the statement of your own wants. In short, you should return to the preparation phase to plan your movement to the proposal phase. Taking a short break is not as difficult as it might seem. Very few negotiations over major issues are settled at a single meeting and using a natural break in those that are is not beyond most negotiators to suggest or arrange.

CHECKLIST FOR SIGNALLING

- Are there are signs of potential movement in the debate?
- What signals have you made to indicate your own willingness to consider moving?
- If they have been ignored, how might you reword them?
- What is the cause of the other party's "stonewalling"? Confidence, or lack of it?
- Test "stonewalling" by a specific signal linked to a direct call for them to reciprocate
- If there is still no response you can:
  —suspend the negotiation
  —require them to seek authority to revise their position
- Avoid making unilateral concessions in the hope that they will respond because this only rewards their intransigence
- Listen for their use of non-absolute and qualified statements of their position, or references to their inhibitions
- Ask them to elaborate on the implications of them (their best move is to seek your commitment to respond)
- Respond positively, but vaguely. For example: "I am always prepared to consider constructive suggestions for improving the acceptability of my proposals"

Memory joggers
—Ignoring signals prolongs debate
—Listen more talk less

—Respond and reciprocate positively
—Reward signals not intransigence

Common mistakes to avoid

• Ignoring signals
• Moving in response to intransigence
• Not exploring the implications of a signal
• Not reacting positively to a signal

CHECKLIST FOR DEBATE
Avoid the following:

• Mocking
• Interrupting
• Point-scoring
• Attacking
• Blaming
• Talking too much
• Shouting them down
• Sarcasm
• Threatening

Practice the following:

• Listening
• Asking questions for clarification
• Summarizing issues neutrally (and briefly)
• Asking them to justify their case on an item-by-item base (watch for signals)
• Being non-committal about their explanations
• Looking for clues about their priorities and testing their commitment to their positions
• Seeking and giving information

Common mistakes to avoid

- Asking closed questions
- Not listening
- Arguing to "win"
- Not summarizing
- Making mountains out of molehills

5

PHASE THREE: HOW TO PROPOSE

INTRODUCTION

You will be ready to propose when you are able to summarize what the other negotiator wants and when you have informed the other negotiator of what you want. In your preparation you identified the issues and what you wanted. Now you must think about what the other negotiator wants and, if possible, their order of priorities.

WANTS

Competing wants

In stating their wants, they are likely to have revealed their entry positions. This gives you crucial information. By comparing their wants with yours and the respective entry points, you can see at a glance what, if any, wants you have in common, which of your respective wants are in direct competition with each other, and which individual wants are not contested by either of you.

Proposal language

Your opponent's initial proposal will be a statement of their ideal position. You can judge the flexibility of their position by the language used: "I must insist on . . . /I was hoping for . . . ."

Differing Entry and Exit points

Wants normally have different entry points and the question is whether or not there is an overlap in your exit points (see diagram below). For example, if the most the

buyer will pay is less than (i.e. does not overlap with) the
least the seller will accept, they are unlikely to reach agreement unless one or both changes their exit points. The fact
that their entry points are different is not important—we
expect negotiators to enter some distance from where they
intend to settle.

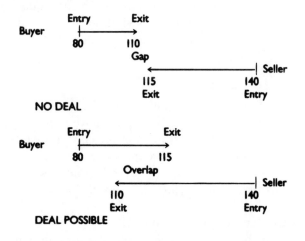

Competing and Compatible Wants

Competitive wants often dominate the negotiations. You
want a high price, the buyer wants a low price; you prefer
to limit your liability, they prefer that you accept conse-
quential loss.

Compatible wants are those where it is in your common
interest to agree—you both want a workable safety policy,
that enables you to protect your employees, them to protect their members.

The existence of compatible wants can help reconcile
differences in the competing wants. By trading movement
between the wants we can avoid a competitive deadlock,
particularly where the negotiators signal agreement in the
compatible want of high priority.

New issues emerge in debate

New issues, emerging through the medium of debate, can be those which you have not so far considered, or which are only of interest to the other party. The latter are the most useful; relatively unimportant to you, but essential to them. These wants can be invaluable in subsequent proposing and bargaining and it is vital not to concede them unilaterally. They can form the crucial item in our trade in wants.

What is a proposal?

A proposal is a tentative answer to the question: which wants of the other negotiator might I have to meet if I am to get what I want? Therefore, a proposal is more effective if it is conditional: "If you give me some of my wants, then I could give you some of your wants." It conveys the tentative terms upon which you might do business.

The two elements of a proposal

A proposal consists of two elements: the condition and the offer. The condition states what you want from the other negotiator and the offer states what you might trade in return.

Make proposals conditional

Proposals are more effective when they are conditions "If . . . then:" "If you consider my concerns then I will consider your concerns."

A tentative conditional proposal will give you an advantage by leaving you room to maneuver in later stages of the negotiating process. If you concede when proposing, bargaining will be much more difficult.

Condition only

A proposal that consists only of a condition demands that the other negotiator gives in. The statement "You will pay in advance" could cause offense by its abruptness and apparent lack of an offer of anything in return.

Offer only
A proposal consisting only of an offer is a unilateral concession to the other party's demands. "We will give you a discount of 15 per cent" might result in the other side's goodwill, but is more likely to provoke further demands. If you will give 15 per cent for nothing, what else will you concede under real pressure?

VAGUE OR SPECIFIC?
Your condition may be vague or specific, but your offer must always be vague, though expressed firmly:

- "If you could improve your delivery schedules then I could consider minimum volume orders"
- "If you could improve your delivery schedules by three days then I could consider minimum volume orders"

Why should proposed offers always be vague?
Why? Because for as long as it is not clear what proposal will be acceptable it is necessary to have some flexibility. The vagueness of the offer does precisely that—it leaves you room for movement without giving in. You offer to "consider/look at/re-think" the acceptability of the other party's wants, or you might offer to "find a way to do something about" this or that want.

Degree of flexibility?
Flexibility is the extent to which you are prepared to move from your initial position. Too little flexibility could give the impression that you are unwilling to negotiate at all, causing the other party to abandon negotiations. Alternatively, too much will signal that you are not committed to your position and you will not be taken seriously. The

answer is to retain sufficient flexibility to revise your position upwards or downwards when necessary.

HOW TO MAKE A PROPOSAL

State what your proposal is. Then stop talking. Make sure you do not interrupt the silence—you could end up making unnecessary concessions or diverting attention from your proposal to your explanations. Silence will put the other negotiator under pressure. You have seized the initiative—it's up to them to justify their contention that your proposal is unacceptable.

Either/or proposal

This is a variation which has certain advantages. By giving the other party a choice between proposals you reduce the likelihood that they will instantly accept or reject, and by the choices they make you will gain a further insight into their position.

RESPONDING TO A PROPOSAL

You do not expect a "Yes" to a proposal, although even if you do get a "Yes" there is still a lot of work to do. You will then be required to specify the actual content of your hitherto vague offer. An affirmative reply to your proposal only suggests that the other party is at least interested in exploring the exchange you have suggested.

Use questions to respond to a proposal

Questions are the most effective response to a conditional proposal, either to question the condition, or to uncover details of the vague offer, clarifying any ambiguities or aspects that are not understood:

- "For a discount I would require a substantial increase in volume"
- "What volume do you have in mind?"

Summarize the proposal

Whether you find the proposal acceptable or not, attempt to summarize it. You need not be concerned that merely talking about the proposal makes it acceptable because nothing is agreed until you say it is agreed.

Beware of saying "No"

The most common mistake people make is to say "No" to anything with which they disagree. Not that you should never say "No"—there are circumstances when "No" is sufficient—but an instant negative is often counter-productive. They may not consider that you gave their proposal sufficient attention (remember the need for mutual respect). Moreover, an instant "No" gives insufficient information to discriminate between the absolute "No," in the sense of "never" and the relative "No," in the sense of "maybe, if there were some changes."

Don't respond instantly

In fact any instant response—whether a negative or a counter-proposal—is likely to send the wrong signal: i.e. that you are only interested in your own solution, not the other negotiator's contribution.

How to receive a proposal: a summary

Don't interrupt: a free concession often comes at the end of a statement, and will be missed out; you might also cause antagonism. Don't instantly reject a proposal.

CONSIDERED ALTERNATIVE PROPOSAL

A considered alternative proposal is a considered response to the proposed exchange of wants suggested by the other negotiator. It follows consideration of what has been proposed and exploration, by questioning and listening, of the content of their proposal. It is a considered alternative rather than a direct and confrontational counter-proposal because it embodies, where possible, elements of the other negotiator's proposals into your own suggested solution.

Example—your considered alternative proposal

By questioning a proposal for a 15 per cent volume discount for an unspecified increase in the order, it is revealed that they are considering "perhaps doubling" the order. While the principle of a volume discount is accepted, your concern may be that you could discount your prices and then find that the increased order does not materialize and, moreover, you might consider that a 15 per cent discount is too high. Having considered the proposal and made a judgment about its worth to you, you could make a considered alternative proposal, such as:

"If you contract to take 150 per cent more volume over the next 12 months, then I would be willing to consider a retroactive volume discount of 10 per cent."

Example—the other negotiator's response

Perhaps you are willing to reduce the qualifying volume below 150 per cent, to raise the discount above 10 per cent, and to amend the retrospective condition. That would be for them to explore and to make a considered alternative proposal to you, such as:

"If you make it a 10 per cent discount on current invoices up to when I reach last year's order levels, and then 15 per cent on all orders from then on, then I am prepared to accept the final 15 per cent discount is allowed retroactively."

MIDDLE GROUND

Somewhere between the two converging considered alternative proposals there is a settlement waiting to be discovered.

In general, you trade things of less value to you than to them, in exchange for things of less value to them than to you. For example, when you are thirsty you exchange money for a drink. You value the money at that moment less than you do the means to quench your thirst. If you did not you would keep your money and forego the drink; the person with the drink values your money more than they value the drink. If they did not they would keep their drink and forego your money. The basis of trade is to exchange the money for the drink, or the drink for the money, with both parties gaining by getting what they want from the transaction.

CHECKLIST FOR PROPOSING

- Proposals are more productive than arguments because arguments cannot be negotiated
- Proposals can advance negotiations
- Proposals can seize the initiative
- Unrealistic proposals divide the negotiators
- Interrupting proposals provokes arguments
- Proposals must address the wants of the parties
- Proposals can be used to initiate responses
- Be firm on generalities, e.g. "We must have compensation"
- Be flexible on specifics, e.g. "We suggest $10,000 compensation"
- Do not use unassertive language e.g. "We hope," "We like," "We prefer." Use strong language, e.g. "We need," "We must have," "We require"
- State your conditions first and be vague or specific
- Follow with your offer and be tentative

Memory joggers

- Don't just complain, propose a remedy
- Open realistically
- Move in small steps
- Invite a response

Common mistakes to avoid

- Complaining but not proposing
- Using unassertive language: "I'd like," "We wish"
- Making unconditional offers
- Negotiating with yourself before you meet the other side
- Opening with an unrealistic condition or offer
- Behaving inconsistently in moving your position
- Smothering a proposal in verbiage
- Interrupting a proposal
- Assuming the other negotiator's proposal to be set in concrete instead of being open to negotiation

6

PHASE FOUR: BARGAINING

INTRODUCTION

Bargaining involves making exchanges—giving something up in return for gaining something else. It is the phase of negotiation which can make the difference between a successful and unsuccessful outcome of the process—both parties must pay strict attention to what they are doing in order to avoid making untraded concessions.

There are a number of techniques a negotiator can use to ensure they reach an agreement favorable to their interests.

A bargain conveys the precise terms on which you would settle

A bargain is a specific solution to the negotiating problem: what agreement is acceptable to both of us? A bargain states the precise terms under which you propose to reach agreement, either on a single issue or on all of the issues.

Bargains are always conditional

A fundamental principle of bargaining is to make any offers conditional. Nothing is ever given away for free—everything that is conceded must be traded for something else.

APPROACH TO BARGAINING

All bargains should be expressed in a common format:

• If you . . . then I

For example: "If you agree to this . . . then I will agree to that."

The key words are "if you agree to this. . . ." Without this provision the other negotiator could simply accept the offer without offering anything in return.

Similarly, the nature and scope of the trade-off that you suggest will signal the value that you attach to your offer. It will also show the other negotiator that you intend to concede nothing unless it is matched by a similar effort on their part. Without establishing this conditional approach they may feel that they will have gained any concessions that you offer as of right, or via the apparent strength of their position.

If . . . then—pitfall

Not all the ways of saying "If . . . then" are automatically helpful. For instance, saying: "If *we* agree to your demand, then will *you* agree to ours?" Although this appears to use the "If . . . then" format it is a question not a statement. Bargains state the cost of agreement to the other party and do not merely ask a closed question that could invite a negative response or prolonged haggling.

CONDITION AND OFFER

Like a proposal, a bargain consists of a condition plus an offer. The condition will specify precisely what you want from the other negotiator, if you are to commit in your offer to any of the other negotiator's own precise wants.

Unlike a proposal, a bargain consists of a precise condition and a precise offer. There is nothing vague about a bargain.

Using the approach we have discussed a bargain takes the form: "If you agree to limit compensation for damages to $35,000, then we will issue a credit note to this amount on next year's business."

Use condition and offer together

A condition on its own is an ultimatum and, as such, is likely to be treated less than favorably. Conversely, an offer on its own is a free gift and is likely to provoke a demand for more of the same. Only a conditional precise offer in the specific format of "If you . . . then I" can secure agreement without giving in.

Always lead with conditions

When presenting a revised offer you must not forget to match each further offer with an appropriate condition. Negotiators are sometimes so concerned with getting their revised offer right, and putting it across to the other negotiator, that they forget to place conditions upon it.

Any later attempt to introduce such conditions will probably be treated with some suspicion by the other party involved. They will either be unwilling to take the condition seriously—after all, you have already made the offer—or they will regard it as a breach of convention—a "moving of the goalposts."

Therefore you should always lead with your conditions. You are then in a position to bargain relative to your stated requirements.

A BARGAIN IS SPECIFIC—IT SEEKS AGREEMENT

When you bargain you are actively seeking agreement. A "Yes" response to a bargain is a deal. If there were any vagueness about a bargain it would be indistinguishable from a proposal. You can say "Yes" to a bargain and end the negotiation on the offered conditional terms. In saying "Yes," you are accepting both the conditions and the offer.

"Yes" concludes the negotiation

When you bargain there is no more ambiguity about what you would exchange for what you want. If they say "Yes" the negotiation is concluded and apart from writing up the agreement there is nothing more to negotiate about in respect of the offered bargain.

RESPONDING TO A BARGAIN

Your response to a bargain depends on whether you accept or do not accept the offered deal without further negotiation.

Should you elect to accept it, you merely inform the other negotiator of your acceptance in whatever manner is culturally acceptable. Usually, saying "agreed," or words to that effect, is enough.

Making a conditional counter-bargain

If it is unacceptable in its current form, however, your best response is to propose a conditional counter-bargain containing your amended terms. Arguing is a weak response because it returns you to the midst of the debate phase and is unlikely to produce a revised bargain. You may, nevertheless, return to the debate phase to explore possibilities of movement—by asking further questions or looking for signals as possible areas of renegotiation.

Using instant counter-bargains

It is quite common for negotiators to propose counter-bargains that amend each other's last conditional offer, without a great deal of additional debate on the merits of their cases. Instant counter-bargains are acceptable in the bargaining phase and have much to commend them in focusing the momentum of the negotiation towards its ultimate conclusion.

EXCHANGE OF PROPOSALS

An exchange of proposals could spark off a run at an attempted bargain. The ease with which negotiators slip from a proposal (vague conditional offer) to a bargain (specific conditional offer) often moves a negotiation to a close in fairly rapid order. By the time negotiators are ready to bargain they should have a fair knowledge of what is likely to be acceptable and how far they have to move to trade for what they want.

APPROACHES TO BARGAINING PROBLEMS

- If they do not accept your bargain, remember that arguing for or against a bargain is usually ineffective
- If they reject your bargain, require them to propose their alternative
- If you reject their bargain, try a counter-bargain that changes the conditions or the offer, or both, in your favor
- Repeat your willingness to move towards an agreement

Arguing is a common mistake

The most common mistake is to continue to argue against proposals that you disagree with. By argument alone you miss the opportunity of using a considered alternative proposal—particularly one that incorporates by design elements of the other negotiator's original proposal—to move into the bargaining phase.

Instead of disagreeing in the forlorn hope that they will change their mind on the basis of your arguments alone, you can move them from their current proposal by offering them a precise bargain. This could take the form of: "If you drop/amend/change your conditions or offer in the following way, then I will improve/alter/change my offer in this way."

Deadlock
Just as a proposal beats a deadlocked debate, so a bargain can unblock a deadlocked proposal.

NEGOTIATING SEVERAL ISSUES
Where more than one issue is in contention (the normal case), it is important to abide by two principles:

• Nothing is agreed until everything is agreed
• All issues are linked together

Keep the whole deal together
The first principle effectively guarantees the second. A piecemeal agreement on an isolated issue could leave you short of negotiating room when you reach the later issues. Your problem then would be how to generate room on the outstanding issues without giving in. On the other hand, by keeping the issues linked you have the means to keep the negotiation open until all the issues are covered.

Nothing is agreed until everything is agreed
Hence, by referring to agreement on issue 1 as being provisional, you are able to refer back to issue 1 (or any other issue) as a means of overcoming a disagreement arising on issue 6.

For example: "We are unlikely to make progress on this issue (6) as it stands, but if you would reassess issue 1 and allow me to make a proposal in respect to them both, I think we could find a way forward." Objections that issue 1 has been agreed will require you to remind the other negotiator of your provisional, as stated, acceptance of earlier issues. Remember: "Nothing is agreed until everything is agreed."

The significance of linking issues

This approach could be countered by the apparently logical suggestion that the list of demands, objections or requirements etc. should be dealt with one at a time. For one thing, an item-by-item approach has administrative advantages, if only in the sense of an orderly agenda.

Nevertheless you must, on no account, be persuaded that an administrative convenience implies that provisional agreement on issues in a list shuts the door on all further consideration of the issues when there is deadlock on late issues. All the disputed and agreed issues should be linked together in the bargaining phase.

By negotiating each item individually you could be forced to make concessions on each and every point. When you reach the stage of negotiating any issues that remain you may find yourself having nothing left to bargain with.

At this point you will be faced with either: abandoning all hope of reaching an agreement, and shouldering whatever costs this may entail; or seeking authorization to improve your offer and taking the inevitable criticism from your colleagues.

CHECKLIST FOR BARGAINING

- Absolutely firm rule—no exceptions at all, ever: "Every offer must be conditional"
- Decide what you require in exchange for your offers
- List and place that at the front of your proposal
- Keep all the issues linked and trade off a move on one for a new condition or a move on something else
- Be ready to bring back into contention any previously "settled" issues if you need negotiating room under pressure of deadlock on a point

Memory joggers

- Remember "If you . . . then I"
- Never give something for nothing
- Lead with your conditions
- Keep the issues linked

Common mistakes to avoid

- Unconditional offers
- Asking permission to concede using question proposals: "If I . . . will you?"
- Forgetting to state your conditions
- Separating the offer from the conditions with explanatory comments
- Agreeing to issues one at a time
- Not linking movement on one issue to movement on another

Bargaining possibilities

- They get what they want on your terms
- You get what you want on their terms
- You both get some of what you want on each other's terms

7

AGREEMENT

INTRODUCTION

There are two major pressures which a negotiator has to contend with. The first of these stems from the fundamental uncertainty of negotiating: never really knowing whether you are anywhere near the other negotiator's Exit limit. As a result, you delay coming to a decision about what is on offer at any moment just in case there is more you can get. The other pressure urges you to come to an agreement before the other negotiator has the opportunity to "squeeze" you any further towards your Exit limit.

The longer the negotiations continue the more time you have to extract all the concessions available from them but, by the same token, the longer you negotiate the more time they have to do the same to you.

THE IMPORTANCE OF CLOSING TECHNIQUES

Inexperienced negotiators often find it difficult to know when, or how, to close deals. As a result, they frequently continue negotiations for too long and, in the process, risk conceding further, apparently "minor," points. When taken as a whole, however, these could represent a substantial additional concession. This situation can be avoided by using the closing techniques given below.

Terminating a negotiation is often difficult

You do not like to say "Yes" in case you can improve on the other negotiator's current offer; you do not like to continue saying "No" in case they come up with something you would rather keep out of the discussion. Hence, you dither.

Deciding when to close

It is easier to learn how to close than when to close.

The decision to close the bargaining phase is a matter of judgment, as it is rare for both parties simultaneously to reach their respective Exit limits.

The credibility of your close determines how the other negotiator reacts to it, as they will not know how close you are to your limit.

By closing you are letting the other party know that you do not intend to improve on your current offer and it is in their best interest to reach an agreement with you.

Nevertheless, attempting to close too early can be dangerous: once you have presented your "final offer," and it has been rejected, you could find yourself trading further expensive concessions later on, plus having to do so in circumstances where your attempt to close too early has damaged your credibility.

Have you achieved what you wanted?

It is best to follow the advice of terminating when you feel that you have achieved what you wanted. Hanging on for more risks something emerging that causes a collapse of the deal.

Don't agree too hastily

Being too eager to agree because the other party has inadvertently offered, or appears to have offered, to meet all your wildest expectations is not necessarily a sensible course of action either. Your reaction may draw their attention to the fact that they have been over-generous, or may lead them to believe that what they are getting is not worth as much as they thought it was. They may then look for some way to undo the deal, or, if they have already committed to it, they might still create difficulties during its implementation.

SELECTING A METHOD FOR CLOSING

There are several methods of closing (as detailed below), although two—the final concession close and the summary close—tend to predominate.

Final concession close

Terminates the bargaining phase by proposing a conditional traded concession to clinch the deal. You must carefully judge the standard of concession offered: too big, and they may believe you can be pressurized to concede even more; too small, and it may be too insignificant to bring about acceptance.

Summary close

Remind the other negotiator of the concessions you have both made, and highlight the benefits to them of acquiescing to the proposed agreement. Then summarize what has been agreed and how far you have moved, then call for agreement on the terms you have offered.

Make them realize the extent of the effort you have both put into the negotiation and emphasize the opportunity to reach a mutually acceptable agreement. This method is particularly useful where progress has been difficult.

Adjournment close

Summarize as above and suggest an adjournment for each negotiator to consider the merits of agreement on the current terms. Specify the duration of the adjournment (hours, days or weeks).

Adjournment will allow the other negotiator time to reach a considered judgment of the implications of accepting/rejecting the agreement proposed.

"Or else" close

Summarize as above and call for a decision by a specific date, with an explicit statement of the consequences (for both parties) of non-agreement.

This is, of course, an ultimatum: "Accept the offer or else!" It is likely to provoke hostility in the other party.

"Either/or" close

This is a good approach if you are at your budget limits. You present the other negotiator with a choice of alternative agreements and they are free to make a decision between them.

AGREEMENT CAN BE DANGEROUS!

Agreement to what is on offer is the last step in the negotiating process. It is the outcome towards which all negotiators work. Once it is within your reach, therefore, you feel relief from the tension of the negotiating process and often experience a sense of euphoria. This is a dangerous time. People often believe something was agreed when in fact it was not. Be on your guard. Pay attention to the details of what you agree.

Agree on what you have agreed

It is absolutely essential that both parties agree that they have agreed with each other before they leave the table, and that the agreement is recorded in an acceptable manner. This is the way to pre-empt subsequent confusion, disagreement and hostility.

Each issue which has been subject to negotiation should be summarized, and the summary agreed between the parties. Any terms that could be subject to differences in interpretation should be defined. (For example, generalized terms such as: reasonable, adequate, sufficient, etc.)

For less formal negotiations, a letter documenting the

settlement reached should be sent by you as soon as possible after the close of negotiations.

DISAGREEMENT OVER INTERPRETATION

The consequences of not confirming what you have agreed, even with people you know and trust, can be horrendous. Any form of dispute which arises later on, perhaps during the implementation of the negotiated agreement, could imply unethical behavior on your part, even if you are genuinely innocent. The other negotiator will naturally dispute an interpretation of the alleged agreement that they have later discovered to be to their detriment. Whether openly stated or not, questions as to each party's good faith and real intentions will be raised.

Convincing somebody that they really did agree to what has turned out to be a disadvantageous clause in a contract, even if brilliantly presented, may leave them feeling resentful. It may also leave you with the suspicion that they have been trying to take advantage of you, and neither outcome is good for your relationship.

Agreements should be completely clarified at the negotiation stage

To avoid the possibility of later discord, confirm in detail what you agreed and clarify any potentially contentious points before you leave the negotiating table.

Negotiate what you agreed

If the summary of what you believe has been agreed to does cause conflict, then it is necessary to re-open negotiations until you can find an agreement. A failure to reach full agreement before you implement a deal is as disastrous as trying to implement a deal which has not been agreed to at all.

CHECKLIST FOR CLOSING AND AGREEING

- Decide where and when you intend to stop trading
- Is it credible? Is it too soon?
- Have they identified or signalled that an improved offer on your part on some item will trigger agreement to the package? (If not, you must get all of their objections out before trading any more offers.) If "Yes," consider the final concession close
- Lead with the summary close and then try the final concession close or vice versa
- If you are going for a "final offer" are you serious or is it a bluff? Remember, a final offer increases in credibility the more formal it is, the more senior the person delivering it, the more public the audience, the more specific it is and the more specific the time for acceptance. Bluffing "final offers" can destroy credibility in the current negotiations and in subsequent ones. Do not try to force a "final offer" under emotional pressure
- Remember: "adjournment" and "or else" closes have a greater risk in them than "final concession" and "summary" closes (and "either/or" closes)
- If the close has succeeded: What has been agreed?
- Detail the agreement
- List all points of explanation, clarification, interpretation and understanding
- Try to prevent them from leaving until an agreed summary has been recorded
- If there is disagreement on an alleged agreement recommence the negotiation until agreement is reached again
- If the agreement is oral, send a written note to your opponent of what you believe was agreed immediately after the meeting

Common mistakes to avoid

- Inability to terminate bargaining
- Giving away concessions in the euphoria of the closing moments
- Misjudging final offers
- Bluffing with a "final" offer
- Unconditional closing concessions
- Making large closing concessions
- Not summarizing what has been agreed
- Making inappropriate threats using the "or else" close or the "either/or" close
- Not recording what has been agreed in an acceptable form
- Trying to "cheat" when recording the alleged agreement

8

STYLES OF NEGOTIATION

INTRODUCTION

We do not negotiate in a vacuum. Just because we happen to be deciding something, neither of us need attempt to bargain. You might seek to force me to capitulate. Neither of us need hold to any beliefs in "fairness." You might attempt to exploit me by smart sales techniques, or by playing on my ignorance, or by threatening me with awful consequences if I resist you.

Where does this leave the negotiator, the person who wants to trade to arrive at a solution when up against somebody else who does not?

The style dimension

Negotiators are divided between those who want to take something for nothing (the RED stylists) and those who prefer to trade something for something (the BLUE stylists).

The style dimension is a continuum, with aggressive Red stylists at one end and assertive Blue stylists at the other. In between the extremes there are varying shades of redness, purple and blueness.

Red stylists believe that negotiations work best for them by:

- Seeing all negotiations as "on-off" activities
- Winning through domination
- Believing that more for them means less for you
- Using bluffs, ploys, "dirty tricks" and coercion to get their own way
- Taking something for nothing

Blue stylists believe that negotiations work best for both parties by:

- Seeing all negotiations in their long-term contexts
- Succeeding through co-operation
- Believing that more for you means more for them
- Avoiding manipulative techniques
- Addressing each party's interests using negotiable tradables
- Trading something for something

In practice, the clash between Red and Blue styles leads to varying outcomes.

Varying outcomes
A negotiator can be intimidated into submission by an overtly aggressive Red stylist.

The submissive negotiator in practice gives something for nothing—they give up what the other negotiator wants to take and get nothing back in return for it. They are so determined to reach an agreement that they sacrifice their own wants to secure it. They fear failure more than they fear exploitation.

A negotiator can sometimes achieve something for nothing by stealth and by hiding their Red intentions.

These people are covert Red stylists. They exploit either by design or by accident—they cannot resist the opportunity to get something for nothing.

The assertive Blue negotiator, however, always aims to secure agreement by trading something for something.

In different contexts you might on occasion display behavior from more than one version of a style. For example:

- Whenever you make an unconditional offer you are being submissive
- Whenever you make a unilateral demand, with no offer of anything in return, you are being aggressive

- When you exploit somebody because you cannot resist the temptation, you are being covert
- When you use conditional proposals only (IF you . . . THEN I) you are being assertive

Thus you require a method of dealing with all of these versions of Red and Blue styles. But you must recognize that while some people are predominantly of one distinct style or another (it is not difficult to spot an aggressive negotiator!) the majority of people with whom you will negotiate may not be so obvious in their style preferences and might switch between them depending on how they read the situation.

DIFFICULT AGGRESSIVE NEGOTIATORS

You are bound to feel at least some of the time that almost all other negotiators are being difficult to some degree— they do not agree with your solution and stubbornly persist in presenting their own. Most of the time we manage to rise above our impatience.

But we do have to deal with people who choose to behave in an extremely difficult fashion beyond the temporary irritations of our discovering that they are not overly enthusiastic about our solutions. These people are usually aggressive, bad mannered and threatening.

The problem is that you want to negotiate and they do not. Their solution requires you to give in to them by giving them what they want (all of it) and foregoing anything in return.

Break the connection between winning and intimidation

Not that all negotiators behave aggressively, because they know that the submissive submit to aggression. Many of them behave aggressively because they confuse aggression with toughness. They adopt aggressive behavior because they know of no other method that would get them what they want. And because they find that other people submit to their aggressiveness, they conclude that the aggressive win and therefore they become aggressive whenever they want something.

You have to break the connection between winning and intimidation. If you do not do this, your submission reinforces the high success rate for those who win through intimidation.

You must find some way to grab their attention and assert two things:

1. That you will not submit to their intimidation, bullying or threats and
2. The only two ways that they are going to get anything from you are based on either:
   • The merits of their case
      or
   • Trading something that you want from them

If their case has merits (you are in the wrong on something) it is pointless trying to defend the indefensible—it only fuels their aggression. How you put it right depends on context, but certainly an indicated willingness to put it right is a minimum step towards doing so.

For example, an irate customer can at least be calmed down by asserting:

• That you apologize for the stress you have caused them
• That you will listen to what they have to say
• That you intend to put the matter right

In the absence of any merits in their case (which of course requires that you listen to what they have to say), or a willingness on their behalf to consider a trade, you will steadfastly refuse to be bullied.

Match?

When confronted by a difficult negotiator: you can style match, but it is risky.

In matching you respond in similar vein to the difficult negotiator's behavior.

The danger is that the aggressive negotiator interprets your counter-stance merely as you being aggressive too (he misses the message about merits or trading as your preferred solutions) and concludes that it needs an "extra push" from him to force you into submission. He escalates the pressure and you escalate your response.

This risks a dispute about "who started it," which blocks progress in the negotiations (even precludes negotiations at all) because the answer is lost in the confusing layers of mutual insults and threats and counters.

The outcome depends on what happens next after your bout of style matching.

You style match to avoid submitting to aggressive pressure, but when doing so you must leave wide open the alternative route to a settlement through negotiation. "It does not have to be this way" is a useful common refrain.

Contrast?

Style contrasting is also risky because a contrasting response to aggression could be perceived by the difficult negotiator as evidence of your submission and a justification for their aggression.

Instead of responding in kind to their ill-mannered and abusive behavior you should:

- Speak more quietly than they do
- Speak more slowly than they do
- Give way to their interruptions—but pause for a few seconds each time they finish
- Not join in bouts of swearing
- Not get dragged into attack against ascribed motives

- Avoid defending yourself against ascribed motives
- Ignore all threats

Of course, contrasting responses like these run the risk of misinterpretation. You could be thought of as submissive. But the contrary impression depends on what else you do in association with your contrasting style.

You should repeat the statement—having gained their attention, which will probably mean that you have to re-peat it more than once—that you will not submit to pressure but only to the merits of their case or to the exchange principle.

For a contrasting style to have impact, it is absolutely essential that you respond instantly, positively and specifically, and without rancor for past insults etc., to any and all of the trading moves that they make. This is critical. Delaying your response, being mealy mouthed about it, hankering after punishment of them for their misdeeds etc., endangers the impact of your message. This is particularly true when they make a small signal of a change in tack in the midst of their aggressive activities.

As for their Red moves, you have nothing to gain from responding to them other than to say "no." You must affirm whenever appropriate the two principles on which you will agree to a solution (merits of the case and trading).

Your assertive Blue message will eventually prevail (it is the only way they can do business with you).

To help you to hold the line in what is a most difficult and trying situation, remember that toughness is not a synonym for shouting abuse, threatening and intimidation. Toughness is based on an absolute and patient firmness of purpose.

HOW TO DEAL WITH COVERT RED NEGOTIATORS
The main problem is that most covert Red stylists do not start off with the intention of cheating you (some do, of

course). The majority of occasions when you are exposed to a covert Red who will cheat you are when otherwise normally honest people find it impossible to resist the temptation to do so. The opportunity to cheat appears without warning and, faced with a safe "steal," they submit to the temptation.

Opportunity to cheat
The covert Red and the assertive Blue are easily confused. The fact is that you do not know for certain whether a negotiator will exploit you. They are unaware themselves of how they will act if they are given an opportunity to exploit you.

This puts you at a disadvantage but this is one disadvantage which is an integral aspect of the business of negotiation. If it is any comfort it also puts everybody else at a disadvantage—they do not know if you will be tempted to cheat them. Nobody knows for sure how they will react if an opportunity arises with some person they are dealing with—we all have the potential to be tempted into being covert Red in certain circumstances, and we almost certainly all have succumbed to that temptation in the past.

Hence, you could be dealing with an apparent assertive Blue negotiator behaving just like you.

This person may intend from the start to exploit you or may be unable to resist the temptation. If they intend to exploit you there are precious few clues, if any, in their behavior because their intentions are deliberately hidden (that is why they are covert). In the latter case, they cannot help it when the opportunity arises, perhaps on this single occasion. Their behavior up to that moment is absolutely honest and above-board but they switch to the covert Red role without revealing what they are doing.

Causes of the covert Red problem

Your problem can only arise if you relax from an assertive Blue style and forget to apply the exchange principle based on conditionality.

If you believe that you are dealing with another assertive Blue, you might demonstrate a co-operative tendency in your style and inadvertently expose yourself to exploitation.

If you reveal your expectations—even your interests—believing that it is safe to do so with this person (who is clearly not an aggressive Red stylist) you might create the irresistible temptation for them to take advantage.

If you carelessly offer movement on the implicit understanding that they will reciprocate, that could be the invitation for them to strike.

Examples include:

- You reveal that you desperately require their services—to exploit you they can increase their Entry price
- You confess that your cash flow is desperate—they strike swiftly by insisting (with regrets) on advance payment

Most covert Red responses are accepted by their victims because it is easier to become a submissive Blue, particularly as the covert Red usually dress up their response in such a way as to convince you that they are genuine.

How to test for covert Red with signals

Basically by never becoming deluded that it is safe to reveal your vulnerabilities and by never dropping an assertive Blue stance that everything but everything is traded and nothing but nothing is conceded.

Among the assertive skills that you must practice is the use of signals to test for covert Red intentions in people who might be tempted to cheat.

Signals are Blue moves. A signal addresses the major strategic question of all negotiators: How can we indicate a willingness to move without it being interpreted as our giving in? Signals indicate a willingness to consider some form of movement only if that movement is not interpreted as you giving in.

- From demanding full compensation you signal that you require *some* compensation
- From rejecting a demand as impossible you signal that it would be *contrary to normal policy*
- From rejecting a general principle you signal a willingness to discuss specific instances where it might be applicable

The key is in how the other negotiator responds to your signal. If they trash it, they are revealed to be negotiating as Red stylists. But even if they respond positively to your signal you still cannot be sure about them. Suppose their clarification questions lead you into further disclosures rather than into a positive response from themselves?

In short, no matter what they appear to be, you never know if they are genuinely assertive Blue or potentially covert Red.

Responding to your signals might reveal them to be Red stylists (seeking something for nothing) but it will not prove beyond doubt that they are not covert Red stylists who might finesse something for nothing from you if you carelessly give them the chance.

The exchange principle
What you do in a negotiation is critical to the outcome. You need not always be a victim of Red styles. The answer to Red style behavior lies in your application of the exchange principle.

Every one of us has a Red side because if somebody offers us what we want for nothing, we will surely take it, and taking something for nothing is a Red style behavior. When we get something for nothing no exchange takes place.

Now suppose we make a proposal that only consists of stating what we want and offer nothing in return to the other negotiator.

What is the nature of our proposal? Surely an aggressive Red stylist's attempt to get something for nothing!

Most of us have a submissive Blue side because there are occasions upon which we would certainly offer something and expect nothing in return. Our motivations (love, terror, tiredness, altruism, etc.) are not relevant here.

Now suppose we make a proposal that only consists of an offer (which gives them what they want) and requires nothing at all from the other negotiator.

What is the nature of this proposal? Surely a submissive Blue stylist's free gift concession giving away something for nothing! And when we give something for nothing no exchange takes place.

Thus, these types of proposal by themselves identify the aggressive Red or the submissive Blue stylist. Separately they are unhelpful to a negotiator—Red demands provoke resentment if not resistance, Blue offers provoke exploitation.

But the exchange principle combines the Red demand with the Blue offer and together they become the foundation of sound negotiation practice.

Combine condition and offer together into a conditional proposal and the assertive Blue negotiator is totally protected whatever the style coming across the table—overt, covert or submissive.

Analogously, the two elements sodium and chlorine are poisonous to humans if ingested separately, but they are also the foundation of life (salt) when ingested together.

A Purple style?

Think of the assertive conditional proposal as a Purple style (a bit of Red and a bit of Blue—the proportions depending on the terms of a proposed deal).

Conditional proposals consisting of your Red conditions and your Blue offers are Purple defenses against any Red plays, whether openly aggressive or covertly threatening.

Your imposed conditionality asserts that they cannot get what they want from you without you getting what you want from them.

The exchange principle conditionally stated:

- Blocks aggressive Red stylists from intimidating you into submission for as long as you apply it
- Does not exploit the submissive Blue because being used to giving things away for nothing they get something back through your conditional offer
- Paralyses the covert Red because if they challenge the exchanged principle (you must get something back for what you offer them) they would have to reveal their Red "something for nothing" intentions which the *covert* cannot do
- Is acceptable in form at least if not in its contents by genuine assertive Blue negotiators because they apply the same Purple exchange principle themselves in their negotiations

CHECKLIST FOR NEGOTIATION STYLES

- "More for me means less for you" is a Red style
- "More for me means more for you" is a Blue style
- Aggressive Red stylists take something for nothing
- Submissive Blue stylists give something for nothing
- Covert Red stylists finesse something for nothing
- Assertive Blue stylists trade something for something

- Against aggressive Red stylists:
  - grab their attention
  - assert that you will not submit to intimidation
  - agreement is only possible if based on either the merits of the case or the exchange principle
- Apply the Purple exchange principle to all proposals (IF you . . . THEN I) to protect yourself from covert Red negotiators

Common mistakes to avoid

- Being inflexible when dealing with styles
- Submitting to aggressive Red behavior
- Failing to test for covert Red responses to signals
- Forgetting to link your Red conditions with your Blue offers

9

THE ROLE OF PLOYS

INTRODUCTION

For a lot of people negotiation is about "dirty tricks," ploys and gambits, which are sometimes confused with tactics. However, much of the advice available on ploys and tricks is unhelpful.

While learning about manipulative approaches to negotiation has something to commend it—because any experience of business negotiation will show numerous ploys being tried upon you—refining your manipulation skills has little to recommend it. But because negotiation is an unscripted interaction with no rules, no appeals and no comebacks, it appears on the surface that a manipulative approach is the dominant one and something you must become adept in quickly if you are to do well.

The fact remains that manipulative approaches can be counter-productive if you confuse identifying what some people might try to do to you in a negotiation with what you must learn to do to them.

Books, videos and seminars that teach tactical manipulation suffer from at least three drawbacks:

• You forget the appropriate ploy for the situation
• You apply the wrong ploy for the situation
• The situation was not covered in the program

This could leave you bereft of ideas when trying to develop a negotiation plan or trying to conduct a negotiation.

Does a chapter on manipulative ploys contradict the above? Not in this context. There is a difference between identifying some of the manipulative ploys that may be used against you and encouraging you to become a manipulative negotiator.

A ploy identified by you in the course of a negotiating exchange is a ploy neutralized. Moreover, the fact that you realize they are attempting to manipulate you should alert you to their Red intentions.

Role of manipulative ploys

All manipulative ploys have a single aim, namely to influence the perception you have of their power relative to your own.

Your perceptions of their power and your expectations of the likely outcome of the negotiation are linked together:

- The less power relative to you that you perceive them to have, the greater your expectation that the outcome will be favorable to you
- The more power that you perceive them to have relative to you, the less your expectation that the outcome will be favorable to you

The manipulative negotiator strives to influence your perceptions of their power relative to yours because by doing so he can directly influence what you expect to result from the negotiation.

If you perceive your power to be:

- Non-existent in the situation, you are likely to give in (which happens everytime you visit a supermarket to buy some groceries)
- Balanced with theirs, you are likely to trade
- Overwhelming, you are likely to impose compliance on them (why negotiate if they have no options?)

STAGES OF MANIPULATION

All manipulative ploys can be assigned predominantly to three main stages or tasks in a negotiation:

• Dominating
• Shaping
• Closing

Negotiations generally follow the above sequence.

DOMINATING

In the dominance stage, the manipulator works to dominate you and the proceedings. If he manages to take over the negotiations in this way he can exert great psychological pressure on you. Knowing that this is his purpose should arm you against being taken in by the onslaught.

He might:

• Insist on pre-conditions before negotiating

You must decide whether you are willing to accept the pre-conditions. You can assert that "nothing is ruled in and nothing is ruled out," that you would find it difficult to make progress with "one arm tied behind your back," or that you have a counter-set of pre-conditions, which are chosen to circumscribe his room for maneuver.

• Declare some issues non-negotiable

Issues that are claimed to be non-negotiable can be divided into two: those that are genuinely non-negotiable and those that are motivated by an attempt to weaken your stance.

Where there is some pressing emotional reason for them making some issues non-negotiable, you can assert your belief that the issues should be a part of the eventual deal, but to assist the exploration of what both of you want you are willing to have these issues set to one side for the moment. Depending on progress on the other issues you can raise the non-negotiable issues at a later time on the grounds that they are the only remaining obstacles to an overall agreement.

- Attempt unilaterally to determine the agenda, its order and the timing

Seizing control of the agenda (what can be discussed and the order in which issues are discussed) is a common manipulative device, and not just in negotiations. The difference between negotiations and routine meetings ensures at least a base for resisting this type of manipulation.

Nothing can really be negotiated without the consent of both parties and agreeing what to negotiate and in what order is a necessary part of a negotiation taking place at all. Where the manipulator scores with this ploy it is usually by default.

- Behave in an aggressive Red style

The aggressive Red style can be tackled using the methods in Chapter 8, as can the use of threats of sanctions. There is little point in responding to threats, especially with counter threats, as this feeds the emotional commitment of the aggressive person. One of the most successful techniques for dealing with threats is to ignore them and with deadlines is not to acknowledge them.

- Disdainfully dismiss you, your products, your business, your views

The dismissal of you, your products, your business, your beliefs, etc. is an attempt to provoke you into anger or to belittle you and whatever power you feel you have. Again, by remembering that the purpose of the manipulator's behavior is to affect your perceptions of the power balance, you can disarm the manipulative ploy by not letting it get through to you.

- Try to intimidate you with props (plush offices, evidence of power, humiliating circumstances for your meeting, keeping you waiting, etc.)

As for intimidation through props, you can cope with them by remembering that "all that glitters is not gold." It is when you take on board the subliminal message—this negotiator is too rich and powerful for me to expect too much—that you are making your most serious concession, especially if you start to negotiate with yourself and lower your sights.

SHAPING
In the second stage of negotiation the manipulator works to shape the deal in his favor. Most deals can be cut numerous ways and by shaping each aspect of the deal the manipulator is picking up benefits—often without giving anything in return—that could more appropriately be held on to or traded for something else.

Some common ploys include:

"Tough guy/soft guy"
It does not require two people to play this ploy. It can be as easily (and less obviously) played by one person. He is on your side, he says, but he has people to report to who do not see you in the same light. However, if you give him something here and something there, he will have a better chance of getting the deal past them.

If you believe him, you cut here and there and over there. The deal shapes up into a one-way street—for his benefit not yours.

You can counter with your own "tough-nice guy" routine—you too have difficult people to please, hence you need something back for any moves that you make.

You can also reveal your knowledge of the ploy, perhaps humorously, and refuse any movement without a trade.

Salami

Shaping by cutting thin slices at a time. Unable to get you to move the whole hog in one go, they get you to agree to a little movement here and there. Once that is agreed they expand on the movement they have gained.

You can simply salami back—this little movement costs them this little amount, that extended (bigger) movement costs them this bigger amount.

When a deal is being implemented, salami can take on a vicious form, sometimes called the "nibble." Here the other negotiator tries to bend the deal by nibbling away at the conditions they did not like at the time.

For example, you thought they had agreed to 30 days payment but they keep taking 40 days to pay. Over time the nibbles get out of control and establish legitimacy because what started off as a tiny nibble can become a permanent and expensive shift in the terms of the deal, and by precedent very difficult to reverse.

The best thing to do with nibbles is to stamp on them immediately when they appear, no matter how small the initial transgression. If they agree to pay in 30 days, require a condition that failure to meet 30 days incurs a penalty. If they have no intention of nibbling they will not demur at a penalty—if they do, you have been warned.

Add-on

The possibility of an add-on ploy is always present. You thought the price was inclusive but once you agree to the price, add-ons spring up like weeds. It's extra for this and extra for that. The true cost mounts, which is particularly disconcerting when the add-ons are revealed afterwards when you need some service that you thought was included in the deal.

The add-on is the special favorite of the covert Red negotiator. It can turn a moderately lucrative deal into a virtual license to collect money. Be wary is the best advice. Always ask for a clear statement of what exactly is included in the proposed deal and what is excluded. "What do I get for my money?" is a potent anti-add-on counter.

Mother Hubbard

They love you and your product but cannot reach the price and there is no way round their budget constraint. The cupboard is bare, etc. When done convincingly, you reshape your Exit terms to secure the deal. They get what they want. You get less than you expected.

Counters are difficult—you can test the constraints, for example. But it is probably better to decide early on that if you can make a deal with this negotiator, fine, but if you can't you are perfectly relaxed about not doing any deal on worse than your Exit terms. It is always bad business to cross a bottom line in hot pursuit of an order.

Russian Front

Two lousy alternatives are presented to you, one so horrendous ("go the Russian Front") that you will do (almost) anything else to avoid it. A powerful deal shaper ploy that can knock you right down to your bottom line (and across it).

Well chosen Russian Fronts are really difficult to counter. "Reduce your audit fees, or we go out to tender" is currently terrorizing usually sensible accountants. If you believe they will implement the Russian Front you cut your fees, and by doing so you increase the likelihood of repeated threats by demonstrating its potency.

Generating other options is the only sensible response

to situations where you are vulnerable to Russian Front ploys.

This selection of shaping ploys does not exhaust the library of them practiced by manipulative negotiators. Fortunately, for every ploy there is a counter, but the best defense is to identify the ploy and neutralize its impact on your expectations.

CLOSING
In the final closing stage the manipulator works to close the deal on his terms. He uses time pressure frequently, playing on some notional deadline common to you both or credible to you.

There is also the problem that because one of the important costs of negotiation is the time they take, which prevents you doing other things, the plausibility of getting the deal settled quickly is persuasive.

Rushed deals are bad deals. If somebody is hustling you to close, it might be because the deal suits them as it stands more than it suits you.

For example, he might:

Demand that you split the difference
This gets you halfway across the gap between you both and has a pressing, though spurious, logic about it. If you both move halfway then what could be a fairer compromise? That depends on the nature of the gap between you. Has the manipulator arrived at the gap by falsely padding his Entry position, while you were less devious and are closest to your Exit?

If the pressure to secure the deal accompanies the "split the difference" ploy, it can prove irresistible. To avoid the ploy try to work in gaps that are not easily split. A gap of 10 is easily conceived of 5 each; a gap of 11.3 is not so obviously divided.

Claim it is "Now or Never"
"There is a tide in the affairs of men . . ." Whether it really is the last chance to secure a deal is a question worth asking. The context might suggest otherwise. You can only judge the circumstances as you see them. One question to ask is: Why? Their answers might give you a clue to the credibility of the claim.

Threaten with the "Or Else" close
Echoes of the Russian Front applied to the closing stage. Depends on the content of the "or else" part of the threat. If credible you must make a choice. Perhaps you should be generating options during a negotiation that give you negotiating room? The more options that you have the stronger the position.

   By identifying the likely ploys (and there are many more than the selection quoted above) you can win the battle to influence your perceptions. If you know what he is about it makes it easier either to:

• Counter (every ploy has a counter)
• Ignore (any ploy is weakened by being ignored)

   If your perceptions are uninfluenced by the manipulator you can concentrate on negotiating the issues.

CHECKLIST FOR MANIPULATIVE PLOYS

• All ploys have counters
• A ploy recognized is a ploy disarmed
• Ploys are to be avoided in the interests of longer term relationships
• Ploys aim to influence your perceptions of their power
• Your expectations of the outcome are influenced by your perceptions of their powers
• Check out changes in your perceptions

- Which of the three stages are you in: dominating, shaping, closing?

Common mistakes to avoid

- Ploys, gambits, dirty tricks and dishonesty

10

NEGOTIATING DIFFICULT DISPUTES

INTRODUCTION

Intractable disputes are unlikely to be solved by negotiation—which is why they are intractable. But not all disputes—even some bitter ones—need become intractable. It depends on what the parties do once the dispute is recognized.

There is a continuum running from giving in when faced with a dispute through to using violence to force them to give in. In between there are many alternatives to violence. The parties themselves can attempt to resolve the dispute by private discussion, negotiation, mediation and problem solving. They can appeal to other private third parties for arbitration or for a command decision.

Beyond private parties there are public bodies—the law courts, the government and international agencies—who can settle disputes peacefully. And all signatories of the United Nations Charter have agreed to accept restrictions on their otherwise inalienable right to settle disputes violently.

The three components of dispute resolution are power, right and interests. Power in this context is coercion. Rights are independent standards of fairness supported by law or social conventions. Interests are perceived needs, concerns and fears. These components are all pervasive; they are at present in all disputes.

Most disputes are settled amicably between the private parties without resort to litigation or violence. Time consuming as the private settlement of a dispute—a major cost of negotiation, for example, is the time it takes—they are mostly less costly than litigation or violence.

Some business sectors have endemic dispute relationships. In construction, for example, main contractors drive down prices for work from sub-contractors (often using aggressive Red ploys); the sub-contractors, to make a profit, often skimp on performance (using covert Red ploys); the main contractors, to avoid fraud, delay payments to sub-contractors until they have checked everything; to survive the sub-contractors skimp on their work. The result is an industry riddled with contentious claims for extra work done (and contentious people pursuing them) and counter-claims for non-performance, both of which wind their way slowly through arbitration and legal procedures.

CONFLICT ESCALATION

Disputes can escalate from a difference of opinion over some problem into a major crisis. What begins with some low-scale anxiety ends with bitter feelings of revenge.

The deadening spiral of conflict escalation is at the root of most intractable disputes. Once the problem emerges (perhaps as seen by one affected party) it can pass into a partisan assertion of one group's right over another's. Sides are taken and those who feel the strongest whip up the fears and anxieties of those likely to be influenced.

Polarization leads to militant hostility to people holding a different view, including people from within the affected group who are cast as "traitors," "spies" and "enemies." Soon all restraint is lost. Moderate appeals, and moderate people, are pushed aside as being "soft" on the issues.

Threats escalate as perceptions of what is realistically possible become unrecognizably distorted. The original issue is now shrouded in the history of the relationship of the disputing parties. Whatever one did or did not do, it is impossible to separate the issue from the behavior of the parties.

Intractability reigns, perhaps to the mutual destruction of both parties.

INTERESTS

Interests are fundamental to the negotiator's quest to resolve a difficult dispute. Interests express the needs, concerns and fears of the parties. They are what motivates you to want something. Behind all of your wants in a negotiation stand your interests.

In the Four Phases approach, which concentrates on the expressed wants of the negotiators, little needed to be said about interests because for the majority of negotiations consideration of what people want is sufficient to produce an agreement. Negotiators are able to resolve their disputes (who gets how much of what, where and when?) without recourse to uncovering the interests of themselves or the people with whom they negotiate.

More complex disputes cannot be settled solely by addressing the expressed wants of the parties (and it can take some effort even to uncover other people's wants). This is especially true when they have many competing wants because this reflects the fact that they may have competing interests.

As with wants, some interests are competitive, some are compatible. The task is to uncover them. Leaving them hidden or unregarded removes the chance of using revealed interests to promote a settlement.

THE NEGOTIATOR-AS-MEDIATOR

Mediation usually involves some form of impartial intervention by a neutral third party who cannot impose a settlement but can assist the parties to secure one.

Mediators are often used when the negotiators cannot close the gap between them by their own efforts. Basically, the mediator goes behind the public stances of the negotiators, confidentially assesses their interests and finds out their Exit positions on the issues. Where there are sufficient overlaps or closeness of issues and wants to suggest that a mutually acceptable settlement is possible, the mediator recommends that they try again.

Negotiators find it difficult to rise above the fray when head-to-head in a dispute and for practical reasons there are just not enough mediators to go round, even assuming both parties would consider using a mediator's services or could afford to do so.

The negotiator who understands the process of negotiation and the appropriate approach to difficult negotiators can engage in the unusual role of the negotiator-as-mediator.

The negotiator as a mediator differs from the normal mediator. For a start, the negotiator is hardly impartial and neutral. They are partisan to their own wants and interests. They cannot expect to get behind the public stances of the other negotiator, nor will they be able to receive confidential briefings on the other negotiator's Exit positions.

But faced with a dispute that is heading towards deadlock, if not quite intractability, the negotiator can adapt some techniques of the mediator and apply them to search for a way towards a settlement with or without the other negotiator's knowledge.

To undertake this task, however, the negotiator has to adopt certain attitudes to the role of the negotiator-as-mediator. In particular the negotiator-as-mediator must accept that:

- Both parties have interests that are important for them
- A solution meets as many of the interests of each side as is practicable
- Interests like wants may be traded
- There is likely to be more than one solution
- Some interests will be competing and others will be compatible

This approach helps the negotiator-as-mediator to rise above the fray without compromising his role as a negotiator.

HIDDEN INTERESTS

Getting negotiators to reveal their wants can be difficult enough. Getting them to reveal their interests is no less easy. This is not necessarily a case of the negotiator being difficult.

They may not know what their interests are. They may not be used to expressing their interests or formulating them in any conscious sense. Why should they? Our wants express what we want, our interests why we want it. And most of us do not examine our motives for what we want.

Others may deliberately hide their interests either because they are ashamed of them or because they hope to gain advantage by not revealing them.

Teachers claiming wage increases seldom do so on the basis that they want the higher living standards enjoyed by others. They usually present wage claims as an investment in the future of our children. Others might maneuver against a position on some excuse when they are really against it because it will disadvantage them in some way. For example, an employee might lead a campaign against something ostensibly on its merits when in fact they are jealous of the person initiating the project and the promotion they might gain from it being successful.

The most common reason for failure to reveal interests is the misconception that what they want is actually the correct expression of their interest. Inflexible defenses of positions usually are brought about by seeing inflexibility as an interest when in fact it is merely a position. Shifting negotiators to look beyond their inflexible defense of positions to examine their interests is one way of a breakthrough. The dispute over the occupation of the Sinai desert by Israel became locked into inflexible positions: Israel would not withdraw and Egypt would not refrain from attacking Israel. By examining each party's interests—Israel in secure frontiers, Egypt in peaceful occupation of the Sinai—the parties were eventually persuaded to trade land for security.

The negotiator-as-mediator can initiate exploration of each party's interests by the basic communication skills of the debate phase:

- Actively listening to the other negotiator and looking for expressions of interests (concerns, needs, fear, motives)
- Questioning to highlight interests
- Summarizing to clarify what lies behind specific wants
- Reframing the issues to reveal alternative solutions to interests

Interests and Options
The negotiator as mediator does not focus on the declared positions of the other negotiator. This is a cause of dead-lock. Simply denying people what they want is a negative approach and it can be perceived as being threatening.

By shifting the emphasis on to why they want something (their interests) it might be possible to step sideways round the inflexible position and consider other options.

For example, a local community opposed to a runway extension wants the extension plans abandoned. The airport authorities want to proceed with them. A deadlock ensues. But what are the interests of the local community? Is it no runway (their want) or less noise (their interest)? Can something similar be achieved that does not preclude a runway extension but does preclude noisy jets flying in and out 24 hours a day?

Generating new options is a useful way to break through deadlock. If linked to perceptive assessments of their interests, progress can be made in finding a solution. Having identified an interest, the next important step is to engage with them in searching for other solutions.

To assist this process the negotiator-as-mediator tries to

set standards by which options will be discussed (better by example than initially by precept because the negotiator's motives may be challenged).

A common cause of failure in searching for new options is that of the negotiators making premature judgments about what is proposed or tentatively suggested. Brainstorming techniques are useful here. Separating the process of inventing new options from judging them helps otherwise fragile new ideas survive long enough to be seriously considered, which could mean that they themselves lead to other options which are more credible.

The negotiator strives constantly to challenge the view that the only solution possible is the impossible one that is driving the negotiators into deadlock. Retreating into defenses based on denying that there is a problem with the single option on the table, or asserting that if there is a problem it is not one shared by you, is utterly counterproductive. If deadlock is a problem then the solution that is creating that deadlock is a problem too. A co-operative effort to create some new options is worthwhile for both negotiators.

Values

Putting yourself in their shoes, if only as a mind game—without adopting their positions, but trying to see why they have adopted them—can reveal underlying value differences. Behind interests stand a person's values.

Values are the belief systems that give people their views of the world, how it works and their place in it. They are a long time in emerging and are usually very difficult to shift once they are entrenched. They can be implanted in childhood or by stressful adult experience (the "Pauline conversion" for example, or the traumas of a recession, war, divorce or ecstatic experience). They are inculcated by a community—or lack of one—and by one's personal life history. They guide what the negotiator believes to be true.

For example, the difficult question of repatriated profits

occasionally arises in international relations. The host country is desperately short of capital and wants foreign investment. It wants to hang on to every bit of the investment and sees profits as a drain on its (usually) scarce foreign currency holdings. Its values lead it to believe that foreign capitalists are plunderers of the nation's wealth. So it refuses repatriation.

But this conflicts with its interests—improving domestic added value from the wages of those employed in the investment—and with the interests of the foreign investor (seeking profits from its investment). Hence, foreign investment falls in this country and with it domestic added value. The foreign capitalist sees the potential host country as a greedy and corrupt regime out to exploit the gullible investor. They regard repatriation as the litmus test of the host country's intentions. A clash of wants (added value profits) looms because values clash or are threatened.

In the clash of value the negotiator faces the most difficult of all deadlocks. Any attempts that are perceived to change somebody's values are bitterly resisted. If a dispute can be raised into a struggle of values the spiral of conflict can be spun rapidly into total opposition. This leads to clear advice: Understand a negotiator's values, even study them, but make no moves to challenge them in any way.

This creates problems when we are not sure of the other negotiator's values. This is yet another recommendation for listening to what the other negotiator says, how they say it, the specific words used, the phrases and clichés scattered in their sentences and any stereotypes they let slip out. These will reflect their values.

Be wary of springing to the defense of your own values. It is better to acknowledge the clear differences in values in a non-threatening and non-condemnatory way. This is especially true when dealing across cultures in countries other than the one with which you are familiar. The more you know about the other negotiator's values in a deadlock situation, the more likely you are to avoid the sort of misunderstandings that lead to avoidable disputes.

If you want to do business with a country where you are the foreigner it is best that you remember that your political views are only relevant where you vote, that your religion is between you and your maker, that your moral code is between you and your life partner, that your ethics are between you and your legal system and that what else goes on in that country is none of your business—*if* you want to do business there (and in some unhappy places wish to leave the country unmolested).

Emotions

Of course, emotional considerations are not avoidable. In disputes they arise inevitably from the commitment each negotiator has to their preferred solution. The question centers on how they should be handled.

Recognizing somebody's emotions is an obvious first step to accommodating to them in the sense that they have as much right to feel emotional about something as you do. Telling somebody that you feel something about an event (for instance, an apparent slur) might be enough to prevent its recurrence. True, they might take advantage of your revelation and mock you. This at least tells you what you are dealing with. But asserting the legitimacy of them to have and express emotions in the negotiations might help build a bridge between you.

Negotiators sometimes express themselves abrasively because they feel intensely about something. They might also do this as part of their efforts to dominate you. But the advice given earlier applies. Because you are not going to be fazed in the slightest by dominating behavior you are not going to react emotionally to their emotional outbursts. You need not retaliate with a display of your own. You understand that they have rights to be emotional without you having to agree that they are right to insist on their solution.

It always comes down to what you do next. If you are the cause of their emotional outburst, apologize for the unintended action (remember the merits of their case) and graciously accept their apologies if the situation is reversed.

CHECKLIST FOR DIFFICULT DISPUTES

- Adopt the negotiator as mediator role
- Search for their interests as the motivators of their wants
- Use debate techniques to uncover hidden interests
- Search for their values
- Do not challenge, criticize or threaten the other negotiator's values
- Understand their values as the cause of their motivations (interests)
- Generate new options by refraining from premature judgment of proposed solutions
- Seek agreement on the substantive issues using new options to meet each party's interests

Common mistakes to avoid

- Ignoring the role of interests in generating wants
- Preferring the satisfaction of mutual failure to the successful conclusion of a dispute
- Attacking the other negotiator's values
- Instantly rejecting attempts to discover new options